No Compromise

JIM BURNS

Regal

From Gospel Light
Ventura, California, U.S.A.

Published by Regal Books
Gospel Light
Ventura, California, U.S.A.
Printed in the U.S.A.

Regal Books is a ministry of Gospel Light, an evangelical Christian publisher dedicated to serving the local church. We believe God's vision for Gospel Light is to
provide church leaders with biblical, user-friendly materials that will help them
evangelize, disciple and minister to children, youth and families.

It is our prayer that this Regal book will help you discover biblical truth for your
own life and help you meet the needs of others. May God richly bless you.

For a free catalog of resources from Regal Books/Gospel Light, please call your Christian sup-
plier or contact us at 1-800-4-GOSPEL or www.regalbooks.com.

Cover and interior design by Robert Williams
Edited by Hilary Young

Library of Congress Cataloging-in-Publication Data
Burns, Jim, 1953-
No compromise/Jim Burns.
    p. cm.
Includes bibliographical references.
Summary: Presents fifty daily devotional readings with Bible verses, short anec-
dotes, and discussion questions.
ISBN 0-8307-2912-7
1. Devotional calendars. [1. Devotional calendars. 2. Christian life.] I. Title.

BV4811 .B836 2002
242'.63—dc21   2001057885

2 3 4 5 6 7 8 9 10 11 12 13 14 15 / 09 08 07 06 05 04 03

Rights for publishing this book in other languages are contracted by Gospel Light
Worldwide, the international nonprofit ministry of Gospel Light. Gospel Light
Worldwide also provides publishing and technical assistance to international publishers
dedicated to producing Sunday School and Vacation Bible School curricula and books
in the languages of the world. For additional information, visit www.gospellightworld-
wide.org; write to Gospel Light Worldwide, P.O. Box 3875, Ventura, CA 93006; or send
an e-mail to info@gospellightworldwide.org.

To my daughters,

Christy, Rebecca and Heidi,

*I never dreamed I had the depth or capacity to
give and receive as much love as I have with my girls.
I think about you all day. I worry for you. I pray
for you. I love you. You have brought more
God-given joy and fulfillment to my life than
anything else in the world. Your mom and I will
"be there" for you. I dedicate these stories, insights
and devotions as an act of worship to God, and
I dedicate them to you, my precious daughters.*

Love, Dad

Acknowledgments

Thanks and thanks again to:

Jill Corey. You are more than a coworker and godmother to Christy. You are a special friend and sister in Christ.

Carrie Hicks Steele. I am one of the most fortunate people in the world to have such a wonderful partner in ministry.

Todd Dean. You are the perfect COO for YouthBuilders and a treasured lifelong soulmate.

Bill Hall. In the last year you have given me some of the finest godly advice I have ever received. Thank you for using your spiritual gifts to make a difference in my life. Mary Hall, you are a "mother of the decade" to Wendy.

Cathy Burns. Our daughters may never fully realize the incredible job of mothering you do. You amaze me daily. I love you.

Contents

No Compromise

Day 1 10
No Greater Love

Day 2 12
A No-Compromise Commitment

Day 3 14
Civil War Christmas

Day 4 16
The Message of a Child

Day 5 19
I'll Always Be There for You

Day 6 21
Sexual Purity

Day 7 23
A Vision Accomplished

Daily Walk

Day 8 28
An Act of Love

Day 9 30
Does Your Family Know You Love Them?

Day 10 32
Our Father Is There for Us

Day 11 34
The Power of DAILY

Day 12 36
God Is Cheering for You

Day 13 39
An Answer to Prayer

Day 14 42
You Are Blessed

Servanthood

Day 15 46
What Would Jesus Do?

Day 16 48
You Are the Only Jesus Somebody Knows

Day 17 50
Responding with Love

Day 18 52
The Road to Happiness

Day 19 54
You Serve Jesus by Serving His Children

Day 20 56
You Are a Representative of Christ on Earth

Day 21 58
You Are the Hands of Christ

Discipleship

Day 22 62
Costly Discipleship

Day 23 64
Choose to Be Different

Day 24 67
Who's in Control?

Day 25 69
The Pressure to Compromise

Day 26 71
The Secret of Endurance

Day 27 73
You Are a Daily Gospel to the World

Day 28 75
Your Best Interest Is His Best Interest

Obedience

Day 29 78
Sometimes It Isn't Easy

Day 30 80
Slow Me Down, Lord

Day 31 82
A Hunger for Holiness

Day 32 84
Trust or Worry?

Day 33 86
Goals for Daily Living

Day 34 88
Walking in the Light

Day 35 90
His Way or Your Way?

Jesus Is Lord

Day 36 94
The Uniqueness of Christ

Day 37 96
Open Your Heart to Jesus

Day 38 98
The Resurrection of Jesus Christ

Day 39 101
The Incarnation

Day 40 103
Jesus Is Lord

Day 41 105
Lord, Liar or Lunatic?

Day 42 107
The Influence of One Life

Commitment

Day 43 110
Radical Commitment

Day 44 112
Full Surrender

Day 45 114
Overcommitment and Fatigue: A Deadly Sin

Day 46 116
Try It . . . You'll Like It!

Day 47 118
We Are an Offering

Day 48 120
No More Excuses

Day 49 122
Taking a Stand

Day 50 126
Accountability and Support

Endnotes 128

No Compromise

No Greater Love

Greater love has no one than this, that he lay down his life for his friends.

JOHN 15:13

If you ever need a reminder of how much God loves you and that He sacrificed His Son for you, this story will be a great reminder.

After a few hymns, the pastor stood up and introduced a guest speaker. With that, an elderly man stepped up to the pulpit to speak.

"Three people boarded a boat: a father, his son and the son's friend. They were sailing off the Pacific Coast," he began. "Then a fast-approaching storm blocked any attempt to get back to shore. The waves were so high that even though the father was an experienced sailor, he could not keep the boat upright, and the three were swept off the boat and into the ocean."

The old man hesitated for a moment, making eye contact with two teenagers who looked somewhat interested in his story. He continued, "Grabbing a rescue line, the father had to make the most excruciating decision of his life. Which boy should he throw the other end of the line to? He only had seconds to make the decision. The father knew that his son was a Christian, and he also knew that his son's friend definitely was not. The agony of his decision could not be matched by the torrent of waves. As the father yelled out, 'I love you, son!' he threw the line to his son's friend. By the time he pulled the friend back to the capsized boat, his son had disappeared beyond the raging swells into the black of night. His body was never recovered."

By this time, the two teenagers were sitting straighter in the pew, waiting for the next words to come out of the old man's mouth.

"The father," he continued, "knew his son would step into eternity with Jesus. He could not bear the thought of his son's friend stepping into an eternity in hell. Therefore, he sacrificed his own son. How great is the love of God that He should do the same for us."

With that, the old man turned and sat back down in his chair as silence filled the room. After the service ended, the two teenagers were at the old man's side. "That was a nice story," politely started one of the boys, "but I don't think it was very realistic for a father to give up his son's life in hopes that the other boy would become a Christian."

"Well, you've got a point there," the old man replied, glancing down at his worn Bible. A big smile broadened his narrow face, and he once again looked up at the boys and said, "It sure isn't very realistic, is it? But I'm standing here today to tell you that story gives me a glimpse of what it must have been like for God to give up His Son for me. You see . . . I was the son's friend to whom the father tossed a rescue line."

GOING DEEPER

- The unconditional, sacrificial love of God is so evident in the story and in John 15:13. How can this incredible reminder help your Christian walk today?
- Imagine yourself being in the place of the father in this story and of our heavenly Father in the Bible. How would you feel if you had to sacrifice your own child so that someone else could live?

Further reading: Romans 5:8; John 10:11.

A No-Compromise Commitment

Then he called the crowd to him along with his disciples and said:
"If anyone would come after me, he must deny himself and take up his cross
and follow me. For whoever wants to save his life will lose it, but whoever
loses his life for me and for the gospel will save it. What good is it for a
man to gain the whole world, yet forfeit his soul?"

MARK 8:34-36

Renewal and revival happen when people pray and often when young people take on a no-compromise type of lifestyle for God. Renewal and revival often begin when young people take a stand for God. Great renewal has swept the country of Romania since the walls of communism broke down. One of the most inspiring stories I have ever heard came out of the Romanian revolution.

There were 15 students ages 11 to 18 who prayed and sang songs in honor of God and in defiance of Nicolae Ceausescu, the evil ruler of Romania at the time. When Ceausescu entered Romanian leadership 27 years prior to the event we are talking about, he said, "I will erase Christmas and Easter from the Romanian people. In other words, my goal is to stop Christianity from being practiced in this country."

The kids sang songs of praise, hymns and Christmas carols with candles lit as several hundred adults watched. The Romanian secret police were called in to squelch what they saw as a protest. The crowd dispersed but the students remained singing and praying. The secret police begged the children to stop. Even they didn't want to shoot the children of their city. The students remained firm. That night 15 students became martyrs for Jesus Christ as the secret police pointed their AK-47 machine guns at them and murdered them all.

Two nights later there were over 250,000 Romanian people in that very square singing songs of praise with candles lit in honor of God, and Ceausescu was gone from power. Fifteen martyrs helped change the spiritual climate of an entire nation of over 50 million people.

God calls very few to be martyrs, but he does call all of us to take a radical stand for Christ. With prayer and strong convictions the result is renewal and revival.

GOING DEEPER

- Read the words of Jesus in Mark 8:34-38. How do these words apply to the theme of renewal and revival in the world?
- Again God calls very few to ever be a martyr for Him, but He does call all to a radical commitment. What cross must you pick up and carry to go all the way with God?

Further reading: Luke 14:25-34; Matthew 10:39-40.

DAY 3

Civil War Christmas

The virgin will be with child and will give birth to a son, and they will
call him Immanuel—which means, "God with us."

MATTHEW 1:23

A story has been told of a most beautiful and bold act of love that happened in one of the bloodiest battles of the Civil War. It was 11 days before Christmas. Peace and goodwill were far from the thoughts of 200,000 Union and Confederate soldiers facing each other across the broad, blood-spattered arena of Fredericksburg, Virginia, on December 14, 1862.

The past few days had been gruesome, with more than 12,000 soldiers killed. Nineteen-year-old Sergeant Richard Kirkland had seen enough. Kirkland went to see Confederate General Joseph Kershaw. "General," he said, "I can't stand this! All night long I hear those poor Union people calling for water, and I can't stand it any longer. I ask permission to go and give them water."

Kershaw was stunned. They were the enemy. "Sergeant," he replied, "you'll get a bullet through your head the moment you step over the stone wall onto the plain."

"Yes, sir," replied Kirkland. "I know that, but if you will let me, I'm willing to try it." The general responded, "The sentiment which prompts you is so noble that I will not refuse your request. God protect you. You may go."

Quickly, this young 19-year-old soldier from South Carolina hurdled the wall and immediately exposed himself to the fire of the

Yankee sharpshooters. Kirkland walked calmly toward the Union lines until he reached the nearest wounded soldier. Kneeling, he took off his canteen and gently lifted the enemy soldier's head to give him a long, deep drink of refreshing cold water. He placed a knapsack under the head of his enemy and moved on to the next.

He repeated this process over and over again until well past dark. As one writer observes, "Troops on both sides who watched this unselfish act paid young Kirkland the supreme tribute—not a standing ovation, but a respectful awed silence."

I love this story, because it cuts to the heart of Christmas and the Christian faith. What Richard Kirkland did on December 14 reflects the spirit of December 25 when we celebrate the birth of One who could have remained within the safe confines of heaven, but chose to venture into hostile territory to give thirsty souls a drink of Living Water.

Let all the earth keep silence. The Savior has come.

GOING DEEPER

- What are the implications for your life according to Matthew 1:23, "God with us"?
- As this man offered water to wounded enemies, how does Christ offer humankind Living Water according to John 4:10?

Further reading: Isaiah 7:14; Romans 5:8; John 3:16.

The Message of a Child

People were bringing little children to Jesus to have him touch them,
but the disciples rebuked them. When Jesus saw this, he was indignant. He said
to them, "Let the little children come to me, and do not hinder them, for the
kingdom of God belongs to such as these. I tell you the truth, anyone who will
not receive the kingdom of God like a little child will never enter it."

MARK 10:13-15

I love the lesson this mother learned from her innocent child.

We were the only family with children in the restaurant. I sat Erik in a highchair. Suddenly Erik squealed and said, " Hi there." He pounded his hands on the high-chair tray and wriggled and giggled with merriment. I looked around and saw the source of his merriment. It was a man with a tattered rag of a coat, dirty, greasy and worn. His pants were baggy with a zipper at half-mast and his toes poked out of would-be shoes. His shirt was dirty and his hair uncombed and unwashed. His whiskers were too short to be called a beard and his nose was so varicosed it looked like a road map. We were too far from him to smell him, but I was sure he smelled. His hands waved and flapped on loose wrists.

"Hi there, baby. I see ya, buster," the man said to Erik. My husband and I exchanged looks that said, "What do we do?" Everyone in the restaurant noticed and looked at us and then at the man. The old geezer was creating a nuisance with my beautiful baby. Our meal came, and the man began shouting across the room, "Do ya know patty-cake? Do ya know peekaboo? Hey, look, he knows peekaboo."

Nobody thought the old man was cute. He was obviously drunk. My husband and I were embarrassed. We ate in silence, all except for Erik, who was running through his repertoire for the admiring skid-row bum who in turn reciprocated with his cute comments.

We finally got through the meal and headed for the door. My husband went to pay the check and told me to meet him in the parking lot. The old man sat poised between me and the door. "Lord, just let me out of here before he speaks to me or Erik," I prayed. As I drew closer to the man, I turned my back trying to side-step him and avoid any air he might be breathing. As I did, Erik leaned over my arm, reaching with both arms in a baby's pick-me-up position. Before I could stop him, Erik had propelled himself from my arms to the man's.

Suddenly a very smelly old man and a very young baby con-summated their love relationship. Erik, in an act of total trust, love and submission laid his tiny head upon the man's ragged shoulder. The man's eyes closed, and I saw tears hover beneath his lashes. His aged hands, full of grime, pain and hard labor, gently, so gently cra-dled my baby's bottom and stroked his back. No two beings have ever loved so deeply for so short a time. I stood awestruck. The old man rocked and cradled Erik in his arms for a moment, and then his eyes opened and set squarely on mine. He said in a firm com-manding voice, "You take care of this baby." Somehow I managed to say "I will," from a throat that contained a stone. He pried Erik from his chest unwillingly, longingly, as though he were in pain. I received my baby, and the man said, "God bless you, ma'am, you've just given me my Christmas gift." I said nothing more than a mut-tered thanks.

With Erik in my arms, I ran for the car. My husband was won-dering why I was crying and holding Erik so tightly, and why I was saying, "My God, my God, forgive me." I had just witnessed Christ's love shown through the innocence of a tiny child who saw no sin, who made no judgment . . . a child who saw a soul, and a mother who saw a suit of clothes. I was a Christian who was blind, holding a child who was not. I felt it was God asking "Are you willing to share your son for a moment?" when He shared His for eternity. The ragged old man, unwittingly, had reminded me that to enter the kingdom of God, we must become as little children.

GOING DEEPER

- The simple faith of a child is always a most inspiring experience. What do you think it means for your life to take on more of the message of Jesus in Mark 10:14-15?
- How can you take on a childlike faith today? What specifically is missing in your life of faith that perhaps was more present in your life as a child?

Further reading: Mark 9:36-37; Matthew 18:1-6.

I'll Always Be There for You

Keep your lives free from the love of money and be content with what you have,
because God has said, "Never will I leave you; never will I forsake you."

HEBREWS 13:5

A parent's unconditional love is often the closest illustration we have of the "I will never leave you nor forsake you" kind of love from God. Yet even a parent's love pales compared to the depth, breadth and integrity of God's love and passion for you. I love how one of my favorite authors, Max Lucado, describes this kind of love in a story about a father, a son, a tragedy and a great victory.

The 1989 Armenian earthquake needed only four minutes to flatten the nation and kill thirty thousand people. Moments after the deadly tremor ceased, a father raced to an elementary school to save his son. When he arrived, he saw that the building had been leveled. Looking at the mass of stones and rubble, he remembered a promise he had made to his child: "No matter what happens, I'll always be there for you." Driven by his own promise, he found the area closest to his son's room and began to pull back the rocks. Other parents arrived and began sobbing for their children. "It's too late," they told the man, "You know they are dead. You can't help." Even a police officer encouraged him to give up.

But the father refused. For eight hours, then sixteen, then thirty-two—for thirty-six hours he dug. His hands were raw and his energy gone, but he refused to quit. Finally, after thirty-eight wrenching hours he pulled back a boulder and heard his son's voice. He called his boy's name, "Arman! Arman!" And a voice answered him, "Dad, it's me!" The boy added these priceless words, "I told the other kids not to worry. I told them if you were alive, you'd save me, and when you saved me, they'd be saved, too. Because you promised me, 'No matter what I'll always be there for you.'"[1]

GOING DEEPER

- Can you imagine your heavenly Father possessing this kind of passion for you, His child? He does! Read Hebrews 13:5 and let the words sink in about what it means for your life.
- What does it mean for God to never leave you nor forsake you when problems and struggles still come to all humans?

Further reading: Deuteronomy 31:5-8; 1 John 4:10.

DAY 6

Sexual Purity

Flee from sexual immorality. All other sins a man commits are outside his body, but he who sins sexually sins against his own body. Do you not know that your body is a temple of the Holy Spirit, who is in you, whom you have received from God? You are not your own; you were bought at a price. Therefore honor God with your body.

1 CORINTHIANS 6:18-20

When our daughter was 15, my wife, Cathy, and I took her out for a nice dinner to read the above Scripture to her and discuss sexual purity. Today she wears a purity pledge ring as a symbol of the important decision she made that night to remain sexually pure. I'm sure she will need to recommit to purity many other times until she gets married, and frankly, even after she gets married, like the rest of Christian adults who continue to strive for sexual purity. Here was her prayer of commitment:

The Sexual Purity Pledge
Believing that God's best for my life and others is to keep my life sexually pure and refrain from sexual intercourse until the day I enter marriage, I commit my body to God, my future mate and my family.

Duncan Doanty 7/10/04
Signature and date

According to today's Scripture, all Christians are challenged to strive to live lives of sexual purity. This of course includes not only issues like adultery and fornication, but also the important issues of pornography, media, music and anything else that would take our minds off God's best and onto things of the world.

To choose to be sexually pure in today's society is not easy. You will definitely need to take the sound advice the apostle Paul gave to the Romans almost 2,000 years ago, "Therefore, I urge you, brothers, in view of God's mercy, to offer your bodies as living sacrifices, holy and pleasing to God—this is your spiritual act of worship. Do not conform any longer to the pattern of this world, but be transformed by the renewing of your mind. Then you will be able to test and approve what God's will is—his good, pleasing and perfect will" (Rom. 12:1-2).

Are you ready once again, or for the first time, to give your mind and body to God today? Thousands of people have regretted not giving their bodies and minds to God. I don't know anyone who has ever regretted striving for purity.

GOING DEEPER

- Read 1 Corinthians 6:19-20. According to verse 19, how can you radically respect the opposite sex? What do you think it means to give God your body?
- Are you ready to take the Sexual Purity Pledge? If so, take a few moments to pray a prayer of commitment to God, and sign the pledge in today's devotion.

Further reading: 1 Thessalonians 4:3-6; Philippians 4:8.

A Vision Accomplished

His master replied, "Well done, good and faithful servant! You have been faithful with a few things; I will put you in charge of many things. Come and share your master's happiness!"

MATTHEW 25:21

Chris was a no-compromise kind of Christian high school student with an incredible vision to share the good news of Jesus Christ with every high school student at Dunwoody High School in Atlanta. As a senior, he shared this vision with his youth pastor, Andy Stanley. Even Andy was humbled by this kind of goal and this kind of faith. Chris kept praying and believing. His entire senior year he remained faithful to the Lord and looked for every possibility to share the gospel with people at his school. One day he met a brand-new student named Mark. Mark had just moved to Atlanta from Florida to live with his dad after his mom basically couldn't handle him anymore. Mark was angry and packed a major negative attitude. Chris didn't care. He found some things in common and invited Mark to come over to his house to listen to music. Before the night was over Mark had opened up to Chris, admitting he was pretty much mad at the world and that his drug and alcohol abuse was a potential problem.

Chris listened carefully and then told him that God loved him in spite of all he had done. That night Chris introduced Mark to the eternal hope found in Jesus. The school year came and went, and Chris never had the opportunity to present the gospel to the entire student body, which had been his goal.

The next year Mark, who was now a senior, came running excitedly into Andy's youth group. He told Andy that the principal of his school had asked him to speak to the entire student body at an assembly right before spring break. The school officials were concerned about all the drug and alcohol abuse. They were bringing in a special professional speaker but wanted Mark to speak for a few minutes after the main presentation.

Mark was very nervous as he made his way up to the podium in front of every student in his school. He took the microphone off the stand and said, "When I first came to Dunwoody High School, I hated everything and everybody." He talked about his life in Florida. He shared his intense anger. He delved into his experience with alcohol and drugs. The entire student body was absolutely quiet. You could have heard a pin drop. Then Mark turned the corner. "One day a guy named Chris Folley introduced himself to me and invited me to his house. That night I told him about my life and my hatred for everything and everybody. He listened and then told me about the love of God found in a relationship with Jesus Christ. That night I prayed with Chris and my life changed."

The students rose to their feet and gave Mark a standing ovation. Although Chris Folley was now in college, I wonder if he later heard that God had answered his prayer, and that his vision to speak to the entire student body of Dunwoody High School had been accomplished through someone he had introduced to Jesus—Mark.

Don't be surprised if God plants a vision in your heart, and then through your no-compromise faithfulness fulfills it in a greater way than you ever imagined.

GOING DEEPER

- What is the principle according to Matthew 25:21? If you need help understanding this principle read the entire

25th chapter of Matthew. How can it radically affect your life in a positive way?

• What acts of faithfulness is God calling you to do today?

Further reading: Luke 16:10; Deuteronomy 5:33.

Daily Walk

An Act of Love

A new command I give you: Love one another. As I have loved you,
so you must love one another. By this all men will know that you are my
disciples, if you love one another.

JOHN 13:34-35

At one of the Special Olympics recently, nine runners took off in the 100-yard dash. The leader in the race fell while he was running and skinned his knee. Then an amazing sight took place. All the other kids ran past the young man who had been out in front, but when they heard him crying they all stopped and went back to comfort him. One of the little girls kissed his knee to make him feel better. After they helped him up they all linked arms. The children finished the race as one—arms linked together.

The crowd gave them a standing ovation, cheering and crying for these incredibly giving kids. Perhaps in those special moments those kids taught us all a lesson about what it is to love one another and truly be a friend. What can you do today to show genuine love and support to someone else?

GOING DEEPER

• In John 13:34-35 Jesus challenged his disciples to show the world that there is a God who loves them by the love the disciples had for one another. How do you see this principle working in your own life?

- Who can you go out of your way to show the love of God to today? What act of kindness and love will you offer?

Further reading: John 15:12-13; 1 John 3:11-18.

Does Your Family Know You Love Them?

He will turn the hearts of the fathers [and mothers] to their children, and the hearts of the children to their fathers [and mothers]; or else I will come and strike the land with a curse.

MALACHI 4:6

My mother had been very sick with cancer. We knew she was going to die. Over the months of her sickness my mom and I had some very special talks about life, God and our family. My emotions were often raw. I would laugh harder and cry harder than I ever had before.

My mom's body was shutting down. It was only a matter of time. Most every day, as her youngest son, I would find the time out of the busyness of life to sit with her, since she was confined to her hospice-care bed. That July, I was struggling with the idea of having to leave my mom's bedside to go and speak to 6,000 students in Colorado at an international denominational youth event. The day before I was to leave, my mom seemed to be doing better than she had for many weeks. She told me, "Go and speak to the kids, and I will be right here when you get back." Hesitantly, I decided she was right. As I left the room she called out to me in a very weak voice, "Jimmy, I love you!"

"I love you too, Mom."

I left for Colorado and spoke to the students. After the evening event at the conference, I came back to my hotel room, and there was a message to call my wife. Cathy told me that my mom had died.

I was crushed that I had not been there with her. After a restless night of thoughts, tears and prayers, I left for the airport, and then it dawned on me. The last words my mother ever said to me were "I love you, Jimmy." The last words I ever said to her were, "I love you too, Mom." What a blessing!

How is your relationship with your family? Is there an atmosphere of love and warmth, or is there some hostility? Whatever your relationship is like with your family, the biblical mandate is to be loving and supportive. God's vehicle for faith and love is often a family. Who do you need to say "I love you" to today?

GOING DEEPER

- The very last verse of the Old Testament is Malachi 4:6. What do you think that verse means for today's generation? For your own family relationships?
- Who is on your list of family members or close friends who could use an expression of warmth and love from you today? What will you tell them? If you can't say it in person, write a note or an e-mail, or pick up the phone.

Further reading: Proverbs 3:3-4; Psalm 85:10.

Our Father Is There for Us

The LORD himself goes before you and will be with you; he will never leave you nor forsake you. Do not be afraid; do not be discouraged.

D E U T E R O N O M Y   3 1 : 8

Derek Redmond was a 26-year-old Briton, favored to win the 400-meter race in the 1992 Barcelona Olympics. Halfway into his semi-final heat, a fiery pain seared through his right leg. He crumpled to the track with a torn hamstring.

As the coaches and medical attendants were approaching, Redmond fought to his feet. "It was animal instinct," he would later say. He set out hopping, pushing away the coaches in a crazed attempt to finish the race.

When he reached the stretch, a big man pushed through the crowd. He was wearing a T-shirt that read "Have you hugged your child today?" and a hat that challenged "Just Do It." The man was Jim Redmond, Derek's father.

"You don't have to do this," he told his weeping son.

"Yes, I do," Derek declared.

"Well, then," said Jim, "we're going to finish this together."

And they did. Jim wrapped Derek's arm around his shoulder and helped him hobble to the finish line. Fighting off security men, the son's head sometimes buried in the father's shoulder, they stayed in Derek's lane to the end.

The crowd clapped, then stood, then cheered, and then wept as the father and son finished the race. He obviously didn't win the Olympics, but there was not a dry eye in the crowd.

What made the father do it? What made the father leave the stands to meet his son on the track? Was it the strength of his child? No, it was the pain of his child. His son was hurt and fighting to complete the race. So the father came to help him finish.

God does the same. Our prayers may be awkward. Our attempts may be feeble. But since the power of prayer is in the One who hears it and not the one who says it, our prayers do make a difference. And our heavenly Father puts His holy arms around us and reminds us that life may not be easy, but He will be there for us.

GOING DEEPER

- How does Deuteronomy 31:8 make you feel about God's commitment to you?
- The power of prayer is not in the one who says it (you), but rather in the One who hears it (God). How does this statement apply to your life?

Further reading: Deuteronomy 31:6; Hebrews 13:5.

The Power of DAILY

This is the day the LORD has made; let us rejoice and be glad in it.

PSALM 118:24

An unbalanced (or undisciplined) life will not be kind to us in the areas we neglect. The secret to living a vibrant and no-compromise faith is in the power of DAILY. Daily we are to come to God and renew our commitment and relationship. He will give us the strength to live daily for Him. Daily we can recognize His lordship in our life, and daily we will find the power to live for God. Here is a simple but excellent way to remember the truth of the power of DAILY.

Decide to Follow God Daily

>   Discipline yourself for the purpose of godliness (see 1 Tim. 4:7).

Adore and Praise God Daily

>   The Lord inhabits our praise (see Ps. 22:3).

In the Word Daily

>   The word is a lamp to your feet and a light for your path (see Ps. 119:105).

Love Others Daily

>   This is the message you heard from the beginning: You should love one another (see 1 John 3:11).

Yahweh Reigns

>   The Lord reigns forever (see Ps. 146:10).

GOING DEEPER

- Read Psalm 118:24, and then write out how it applies to your life today.
- What specific steps can you take today to live out the power of DAILY in your life?

Further reading: Matthew 6:34; Luke 11:3.

God Is Cheering for You

Yet to all who received him, to those who believed in his name,
he gave the right to become children of God.

JOHN 1:12

One of my favorite inspirational stories is about a young man who went to college and tried out for the football team as a walk-on. Everyone was sure he could never make the cut, but he did.

The coach admitted that he kept him on the roster because he always put his heart and soul into every practice, and at the same time provided the other members with the spirit and hustle they badly needed. The news that he had survived the cut thrilled the young man so much that he rushed to the nearest phone and called his father. He was an only child and had grown up in a small town, living with just his father.

His dad was so proud of his son and was sent season tickets for all the games. This persistent young athlete never missed practice during his four years at college, but he never got to play in the game.

It was the end of his senior football season, and as he trotted onto the practice field shortly before the big play-off game, the coach met him with a telegram. The young man read the telegram, and he became deathly silent. Then, swallowing hard, he mumbled to the coach, "My father died this morning. Is it all right if I miss practice today?" The coach put his arm gently around his shoulder and said, "Take the rest of the week off, son. And don't even plan to come back to the game on Saturday."

Saturday arrived, and the game was not going well.

In the third quarter, when the team was 10 points behind, a silent young man quietly slipped into the empty locker room and put on his football gear. As he ran onto the sidelines, the coach and his players were astounded to see their faithful teammate back so soon. "Coach, please let me play. I've just got to play today," said the young man. The coach pretended not to hear him. There was no way he wanted his worst player in this close play-off game. But the young man persisted, and finally, feeling sorry for the kid, the coach gave in.

"All right," he said. "You can go in." Before long, the coach, the players and everyone in the stands could not believe their eyes. This little unknown, who had never played before, was doing everything right. The opposing team could not stop him. He ran, passed, blocked and tackled like a star. His team began to triumph. The score was soon tied. In the closing seconds of the game, this kid intercepted a pass and ran all the way for the winning touchdown. The fans broke loose. His teammates hoisted him onto their shoulders. Such cheering you never heard!

Finally, after the stands had emptied and the team had showered and left the locker room, the coach noticed that the young man was sitting quietly in the corner all alone. The coach came to him and said, "Son, I can't believe it. You were fantastic! Tell me what got into you? How did you do it?"

He looked at the coach, with tears in his eyes, and said, "Well, you knew my dad died, but did you know that my dad was blind?" The young man swallowed hard and forced a smile, "Dad came to all my games, but today was the first time he could see me play, and I wanted to show him I could do it!"

Like the athlete's father, God is always there cheering for us, always reminding us to go on. God even offers us a hand, for God knows what is best and is willing to give us what we need and not simply what we want. God has never missed a single game. What a joy to know that life is meaningful if lived for the Highest. Live for God, who's watching us in the game of life.

GOING DEEPER

- How does this story remind you of God's love for you?
- How does John 1:12 apply to your life?

Further reading: Psalm 139:13-16; Ephesians 5:1.

An Answer to Prayer

*Jesus replied, "I tell you the truth, if you have faith and do not doubt,
not only can you do what was done to the fig tree, but also you can say to this
mountain, 'Go, throw yourself into the sea,' and it will be done. If you
believe, you will receive whatever you ask for in prayer."*

MATTHEW 21:21-22

My friend Kevin Dyer is a missionary around the world. He tells a beautiful story of an experience another medical missionary had in Central Africa.

"One night I had worked hard to help a mother in the labor ward, but in spite of all we could do she died, leaving us with a very tiny, premature baby and a crying two-year-old daughter. We would have difficulty keeping the baby alive. We had no incubator. We had no electricity to run an incubator, and we had no special feeding facilities. Although we lived on the equator, nights were often chilly with treacherous drafts. A student midwife went for the box we had for such babies and for the cotton wool that the baby would be wrapped in. Another went to stoke the fire and fill a hot-water bottle. She came back shortly, in distress, to tell me that in filling the hot-water bottle it had burst. 'Rubber perishes easily in tropical climates, and it is our last hot-water bottle,' she exclaimed. They do not grow on trees, and there are no drugstores down the forest path, so I said, 'Put the baby as near the fire as you safely can, then sleep between the baby and the door to keep it free from drafts. Your job is to keep the baby warm.'

"The following noon, as I did on most days, I went to have prayer with the many orphaned children. I gave the children various suggestions for prayer and told them about the tiny baby. I also told them we had no hot-water bottle to keep the baby warm, and I told them about the two-year-old girl who was crying because her mother had died. During the prayer time, one 10-year-old girl, Ruth, prayed with the characteristic bluntness of African children: 'Please God, send us a water bottle. It will be no good tomorrow, as the baby will be dead, so please send it this afternoon.' I gasped at her request, but she went on, 'And while You are at it, would You please send a doll for the little girl so she will know You really love her.' I was really on the spot now. Could I honestly say Amen to this prayer? I just knew there was no hope for an answer. The only possible way He could answer her request was by sending a parcel from the homeland. I had been in Africa for four years at that time, and I had never received a parcel from home. Anyway, if anyone did send a parcel, who would put a hot-water bottle in it, since I lived on the equator.

"Halfway through the afternoon, while I was teaching in the nurse's training school, a message was sent that there was a car at my front door. By the time I reached home the car had gone, but there on my front porch was a 22-pound package. I felt tears well up in my eyes. I sent for the children, and together we carefully pulled off the string and wrapping paper. There were 34 pairs of eyes focused on the large cardboard box.

"From the top I lifted out brightly colored knitted sweaters. Eyes sparkled as I gave them out. Then there were some knitted bandages for the leprosy patients and a box of raisins for some cookies. As I put my hand in again, I felt it and pulled it out. Yes, a brand-new rubber hot-water bottle. I cried. Ruth was in the front row and ran forward. 'If God has sent the water bottle, He must have sent the dolly too.' She put her hand in right to the bottom and pulled out a small, beautifully dressed doll. She looked up and said, 'Can I go over and give this dolly to the little girl, so she will know Jesus really loves her?'

"That parcel had been on the way for five months. It was packed by a Sunday School class whose leader had obeyed God's prompting to send a hot-water bottle even to the equator. And one of the girls in the class had put in a doll for an African child—five months earlier in answer to the believing prayer of a 10-year-old to bring it 'this afternoon.'"

"Is there some action that you should take, that could be an answer to someone's urgent prayer? Don't push those prompts away, but obey them, and do them, and so be an instrument of blessing in God's hand. I think the Lord often speaks in quiet ways that often involve a thought crossing our minds. Just take action, don't put it off. Seize the day. And you will be a participant in the answer to someone's prayers.

GOING DEEPER

- "If you believe, you will receive whatever you ask for in prayer" (Matt. 21:22). How have you seen this kind of faith work in your life? Have you seen these words perhaps used in a wrong way? How?
- What are your prayer concerns? Take a few minutes to bring them to your loving heavenly Father who cares so deeply for you and your welfare.

Further reading: Matthew 7:7; 1 Corinthians 13:2; Luke 17:6.

DAY 14

You Are Blessed

Blessed are those who dwell in your house;
they are ever praising you. Blessed are those whose strength is in you,
who have set their hearts on pilgrimage.

PSALM 84:4-5

If you own just one Bible, you are abundantly blessed. One-third of the world does not have access to even one.

If you woke up this morning with more health than illness, you are more blessed than the million who will not survive the week.

If you have never experienced the danger of battle, the loneliness of imprisonment, the agony of torture or the pangs of starvation, you are ahead of 500 million people around the world.

If you attend a church meeting without fear of harassment, arrest, torture or death, you are more blessed than almost 3 billion people in the world.

If you have food in your refrigerator, clothes on your back, a roof over your head and a place to sleep, you are richer than 75 percent of this world.

If you have a bank account, money in your wallet and spare change in a dish someplace, you are among the top 8 percent of the world's wealthy.

If your parents are still married and alive, you are very rare, even in the United States.

If you hold up your head with a smile on your face and are truly thankful, you are blessed, because the majority can, but most do not.

If you can hold someone's hand, hug them or even touch them on the shoulder, you are blessed, because you can offer God's healing touch.

If you prayed yesterday and today, you are in the minority, because you believe in God's willingness to hear and answer prayer.

If you believe in Jesus as the Son of God, you are part of a very small minority in the world.

If you can read this message, you are more blessed than over 2 billion people in the world who cannot read anything at all.

When you look at life with this perspective, you cannot help but offer a prayer of thanksgiving for our many, many blessings.[1]

Going Deeper

• According to Psalm 84:4, what is the natural result of the blessing of dwelling with God?

- Take a few minutes to write out your top 20 blessings on a piece of paper. It will definitely put life in its proper perspective.

Further reading: Proverbs 8:34-35; Matthew 5:3-12.

Servanthood

What Would Jesus Do?

I have set you an example that you should do as I have done for you.

J O H N   1 3 : 1 5

Charles Shelton wrote the best-selling novel *In His Steps*. In the book a group of people decide to take seriously the question: What would Jesus do?

Sometimes I wonder:

1. How would Jesus treat others?
2. What would He do if He were confronted with temptation?
3. Would Jesus gossip? Would He ever gripe or complain?
4. Did He get along perfectly with Joseph and Mary when He was a teenager?
5. How would He treat the opposite sex?
6. What would He watch on TV? What kind of music would He listen to?

I recently spoke at a youth event with 28,000 students in Washington, D.C. On the first day a young girl named Elizabeth came running up to me and gave me a pink WWJD (What Would Jesus Do) bracelet. She knew I would be at the event, and she had actually made the bracelet just for me. I was honored by her gift but I'm really not a bracelet guy and definitely not into pink! She told me she would see me the next day, and because I didn't want to hurt her feelings I decided to wear it for 24 hours. All day I kept staring at the WWJD bracelet.

Later that night after speaking to the students, I went to a restaurant to eat with some friends. We had the crankiest waitress I can remember. Instead of complaining and giving her a poor tip, I looked at the WWJD bracelet and said to her, "I bet you have had a really hard day." Tears welled up in her eyes; she actually sat down at our table and spilled her heart out to me. I even prayed with her at the restaurant.

As I walked back to my hotel, I noticed a prostitute trying to sell her body. I looked at my bracelet and instead of looking down on her, my heart melted for the evident pain she must be in. I stopped and stood across the street and prayed for her.

The next morning I took a jog past the White House. This was a season when I did not always agree with some of the moral decisions of our president. However, as I ran by, I looked at my silly pink WWJD bracelet and felt the need to pray for our leader and the country.

That day I took a little longer with each person I encountered, I prayed more often. I noticed more of the day was about serving and not about me. I sent flowers home to my wife. I told my kids I loved them. Simple things. Probably the simple things Jesus would do. When I saw Elizabeth later that day, I hugged her and thanked her—not only for the bracelet but also for giving me a simple but life-changing message.

GOING DEEPER

- Read the story in John 13:1-17. What is the important message Jesus is giving to His disciples in the Upper Room?
- Who comes to your mind when you think about people and ways you can serve them? What can you do today?

Further reading: 1 Timothy 4:11; Philippians 2:5-11.

You Are the Only Jesus Somebody Knows

I have been crucified with Christ and I no longer live, but Christ
lives in me. The life I live in the body, I live by faith in the Son of God,
who loved me and gave himself for me.

GALATIANS 2:20

There was a soldier who was wounded in battle. The padre crept out and did what he could for him. He stayed with him when the remainder of the troops retreated. In the heat of the day he gave him water from his own water bottle, while he himself remained parched with thirst. In the night, when the chill frost came down, he covered the wounded man with his own coat, and finally wrapped him up in even more of his own clothes to save him from the cold. In the end the wounded man looked up at the padre.

"Padre," he said, "you're a Christian?"

"I try to be," said the padre.

"Then," said the wounded man "if Christianity makes a man do for another man what you have done for me, tell me about it, because I want it."[1]

You are the only Jesus somebody knows. Christ lives in you and will use you to help heal this hurting world if you'll let Him. The priest was willing to become uncomfortable for the sake of a dying man. Sometimes I don't feel like going out of my way to reach out to someone, and sometimes I close the door. There are other times when I realize that I represent Jesus to the world around me and that I touch someone not with *my* love but with His love. And it makes a difference in their life . . . and mine.

GOING DEEPER

- In Galatians 2:20, Paul writes, "I have been crucified with Christ and I no longer live, but Christ lives in me." Do you see Christ living in and through you daily?
- Ask God to give you a person to reach out to today. It could be a friend, another person at school or work or even someone in your family.

Further reading: Romans 6:6; 1 Peter 4:2; Romans 8:37.

Responding with Love

Do nothing out of selfish ambition or vain conceit, but in humility consider others better than yourselves. Each of you should look not only to your own interests, but also to the interests of others.

PHILIPPIANS 2:3-4

Babe Ruth is one of my heroes. He hit 714 home runs during his baseball career. But along with being the home-run king he was also the strikeout king. In one of Babe's last major league games the Braves played the Cincinnati Reds. The great Babe Ruth was no longer as agile as he had once been. His game that day was filled with costly errors and strikeouts. As the Babe walked off the field after a dismal inning, the crowd stood and booed his play.

Just then a little boy jumped over the railing onto the playing field. With tears streaming down his face he threw his arms around the legs of his hero. Ruth didn't hesitate for a moment. He picked up the boy and gave him a hug.

Suddenly the booing stopped and a hush fell over the entire ballpark. In that brief moment the baseball fans saw two heroes: Ruth, who in spite of his horrible day still cared about a little boy, and the small child, who cared about the feelings of another human being. Both had melted the hearts of the crowd.

How is your sensitivity toward other people? Do you take time to care about the needs of your friends and family? Sometimes we get so absorbed with our own personal problems we forget that there is a hurting world around us that needs our attention. The strange thing about it is that when we give love and concern to others, we usually forget about our own problems! Make someone feel special today.

GOING DEEPER

- According to Philippians 2:3-4, how are we to consider others? Why is it good to be concerned about the interests of others?
- Who can you make feel like royalty today? How can you show them that you care about them?

Further reading: Romans 12:10; Galatians 5:26; 1 Peter 5:5.

The Road to Happiness

They came to Capernaum. When he was in the house, he asked them,
"What were you arguing about on the road?" But they kept quiet because
on the way they had argued about who was the greatest. Sitting down,
Jesus called the Twelve and said, "If anyone wants to be first, he must be
the very last, and the servant of all."

MARK 9:33-35

We live in a self-absorbed, self-centered world. That's why there is so much unhappiness in the world. It seems to me that happy people are others-centered people and that unhappy people tend to be I-centered. The Bible constantly challenges us to be a servant, to think of others rather than ourselves.

Albert Schweitzer was a person who knew a lot about serving. He was a missionary doctor in Africa for years. Here's what he had to say about becoming a servant. "I don't know what your destiny will be, but one thing I know—the only ones among you who will be really happy are those who have sought and found how to serve."[1]

If you've been feeling unhappy and unfulfilled lately, perhaps it's time to make an evaluation of your life. Are you I-centered or others-centered? Your decision will affect your destiny. The road to happiness is the road of service.

GOING DEEPER

- What two things does Mark 9:33-35 tell us we must be if we want to be first?
- In what ways are you a servant of all? Ask God to give you opportunities to be a servant today.

Further reading: Mark 1:29-31.

You Serve Jesus by Serving His Children

The King will reply, "I tell you the truth,
whatever you did for one of the least of these brothers of mine,
you did for me."

MATTHEW 25:40

Martin of Tours was a Roman soldier and a Christian.

One cold winter day, as he was entering a city, a beggar stopped him and asked for alms. Martin had no money, but the beggar was blue and shivering with cold, and Martin gave what he had. He took off his soldier's cloak, worn and frayed as it was; he cut it in two and gave half of it to the beggar. That night he had a dream. In it he saw the heavenly places and all the angels and Jesus in the midst of them; and Jesus was wearing half a Roman soldier's cloak. One of the angels said to him, "Master, why are you wearing that battered old cloak? Who gave it to you?" And Jesus answered softly, "My servant Martin gave it to me."[1]

This Scripture and this story bring a chill to my body when I read them. I feel two opposite emotions. I want to run and care for every person I see as if they were Jesus, and I want to run and hide in selfishness and self-pity and not touch a soul with my life. The choice is mine to make. I think I'll try to see the Jesus in each person; I think I'll ask God to help me see, with the eyes of Jesus, each person's needs. How about you?

GOING DEEPER

- Rewrite Matthew 25:40 in your own words.
- List some practical ways you can serve Jesus by serving one of His children.

Further reading: Matthew 10:40,42; Proverbs 19:17; Hebrews 6:10; 13:2.

You Are a Representative of Christ on Earth

You are the body of Christ, and each one of you is a part of it.

1 CORINTHIANS 12:27

God created the world.
He appeared on this earth in the form of Jesus Christ.
He was beautiful.
We mocked Him and killed Him.

He rose from the dead.
He is alive and eternal.
He needs a new body on this earth.
You've been chosen!

You are an important part of the Body of Christ. You are needed to fulfill His work on Earth. Your job is to live as He lived and to love as He loved. One other thing—He gives you His Spirit to get you through your day.

GOING DEEPER

- What is the meaning of the phrase "you are the body of Christ" from 1 Corinthians 12:27?
- Did you know you are the only Jesus somebody knows? Today love someone as Jesus would love them.

Further reading: Ephesians 1:23, 4:12; Colossians 1:18,24; Romans 12:5.

You Are the Hands of Christ

You are the body of Christ, and each one of you is a part of it.

1 CORINTHIANS 12:27

If you are a Christian, then you are a part of the Body of Christ on Earth. It's your hands and legs and mouth that He uses to do His daily tasks in your world.

In Alexander Irvine's novel *My Lady of the Chimney Corner*, an old woman went to comfort a neighbor whose boy lay dead. She laid her hand on her friend's head and said:

> Ah, wuman, God isn't a printed book to be carried aroun' by a man in fine clothes, not a cross danglin' at the watch chain of a priest. God takes a hand wherever he can find it . . . Sometimes He takes a Bishop's hand and lays it on a child's head in benediction, the hand of a doctor to relieve pain, the hand of a mother to guide a child, and sometimes he takes the hand of a poor old wuman like me to give comfort to a neighbor. But they're all hands touched by His Spirit, and His Spirit is everywhere lukin' for his hands to use.[1]

God's Spirit is looking for hands, bodies and minds to use. But He seldom uses us without our permission. We, like Isaiah, have to first say, "Here I am, Lord—send me." That is precisely what God wants you to say in order to start your great adventure of service.

Some people you know will spend their lives totally self-absorbed and will miss the greatest opportunity of life, which is to make a difference in our world.

GOING DEEPER

- Did you know you are the mouth and the hands and the feet of Jesus on Earth? What does Jesus want to say or do through you? Where does He want to go through you?
- Can you say like Isaiah, "Here I am, Lord—send me?"

Further reading: Isaiah 6:1-8.

Discipleship

Costly Discipleship

He called the crowd to him along with his disciples and said:
"If anyone would come after me, he must deny himself and take up his
cross and follow me. For whoever wants to save his life will lose it, but whoever
loses his life for me and for the gospel will save it. What good is it for a man
to gain the whole world, yet forfeit his soul?"

MARK 8:34-36

To pick up the cross and follow Jesus means to be willing to go any-
where and do anything for your Lord. It means that you want God
to do His will in and through you. There is a cost to being a disciple
of Jesus Christ, but the end results are well worth it. I recently heard
of a business executive who said, "I spent my entire life climbing the
corporate ladder only to find when I got to the top that my ladder
was leaning against the wrong building. I have wasted my life with
trivia." Are you passionately pursuing Christ? Don't waste your life
in a trivial pursuit when you have at your fingertips the Lord of life
to guide you into greater depths and a more meaningful lifestyle.

To be a disciple of Jesus means to pursue Him like the pursuit
of a lover in the passion of a romance. Christ is worth your every
thought and breath. In Him you will find your reason for living.
Remember that He gives you His Spirit but wants you to give Him
your body, mind, heart and soul.

Going Deeper

- Reread Mark 8:34-36. What does it mean for you to deny yourself, take up your cross and follow Jesus?
- What will it cost you to truly be a disciple of Jesus? Are you willing to pay this price?

Further reading: Matthew 10:38; Luke 14:27.

Choose to Be Different

I came that they may have life, and have it abundantly.

JOHN 10:10, *RSV*

Once upon a time in a land far away there lived a group of people called the Laconians. The Laconians lived in a rural setting; their village was surrounded by a forest. They looked and acted a lot like you and I do. They dressed like we dress and went to school and worked like we work. They even had the same family struggles and search for identity that we have. But there was one major difference: Connected to the ankle of every Laconian was a brace, and attached to the brace was a strong metal chain, and connected to the chain was a round, heavy metal ball.

Wherever the Laconians went or whatever they did, they carried the ball and chain. Yet no one seemed to mind. After all, they were used to the ball and chain, and no one in Laconia was free from the bondage of the ball and chain.

One day the hero of the story, Tommy, was exploring in the forest after school when he went around a corner, slipped and fell—and the chain broke. Tommy had never heard of a chain breaking before in the land of Laconia, and he was terrified. But he was also curious. As he stood and stared at the broken chain he sensed that something very significant had happened in his life. In fact, he tried to take a step without the ball and chain and almost fell down. After all, he wasn't used to the freedom of walking without this bondage.

Tommy quickly slipped the ball and chain back on his ankle. He told no one of his new discovery. The next day after school this new curiosity drove him back to the forest to experiment with his new-found freedom. This time when he unhooked the chain he walked. Yes, it was wobbly, but he quickly learned to compensate, and in a few hours he was running and jumping and even trying to climb the trees in the forest. Every day after school he found himself out in the forest, free to experience life in a different way from anyone else in Laconia.

He decided to share his secret with his best friend. After school one day he brought his friend to the forest and showed him his new freedom. But his friend responded by saying, "Don't be different! Once a Laconian, you'll always be a Laconian. Be happy with what you have." This response only put more fuel in Tommy's fire. He knew he needed to show all the people of his little village that they could be set free.

One spring day when the whole village was outside, Tommy took the ball and placed it under his arm, then ran and skipped through the town. He wanted to show the people of his village his joy and freedom. Their response was that of shock. They mocked him, scolded him and challenged him to not be different. Even his family told him to immediately become a normal part of the community and put his chain back on.

Tommy knew then and there that since he had experienced this freedom he could never again settle for second best in life. For Tommy, mediocrity was out of the question. He would choose to be different . . . and he was different from then on.

I wrote this little story for people who don't want to settle for second best in life. What is keeping you from breaking the chain and striving to be all that God wants you to be? Jesus said, "You will know the truth, and the truth will set you free" (John 8:32). You don't have to live a life of boring mediocrity. God's desire for your life is to break the chain that holds you back and to give your life to His purpose. You can choose to be different!

GOING DEEPER

- Why is understanding John 10:10 like making a new discovery?
- Identify the parts of your life that are holding you back from all God has for you. What can you do to yield these parts of your life to God's purpose?

Further reading: Romans 5:17; John 3:15-16.

DAY 24

Who's in Control?

What good is it for a man to gain the whole world, yet forfeit his soul?

MARK 8:36

When it comes to our life, we have nothing to say about our birth and little say about our death, but in between these two events most of the decisions are ours to be made. Are you letting life and circumstances control you? Or are you, with God's help, controlling your own life and destiny? Don't let life pass you by when you have the God-given ability to make things happen. I've heard it said:

- You can't control the length of your life, but you can control its use.
- You can't control your facial appearance, but you can control its expression.
- You can't control the weather, but you can control the moral atmosphere that surrounds you.
- You can't control the distance of your head above the ground, but you can control the height of the contents in your head.
- You can't control the other fellow's annoying faults, but you can see to it that you do not develop similar faults.
- Why worry about things you cannot control? Get busy controlling the things that depend on you.

GOING DEEPER

- What is your answer to the question put forth in Mark 8:36?
- Be honest with yourself and God. Have you been striving for the things of this world or after God? Who or what is in control of your life?

Further reading: Romans 6:15-18.

The Pressure to Compromise

What then? Shall we sin because we are not under law but under grace? By no means! Don't you know that when you offer yourselves to someone to obey him as slaves, you are slaves to the one whom you obey—whether you are slaves to sin, which leads to death, or to obedience, which leads to righteousness?

ROMANS 6:15-16

The pressure to compromise our lifestyle is one of the greatest battles that comes our way. We all experience peer pressure, no matter what our age. The pressure to compromise makes a five-year-old scream a dirty word or a 16-year-old get drunk at a party. The same pressure forces a business executive to cheat on a business deal, and then say "Everyone does it." A Christian is called to stand firm and not be seduced by peer pressure, even though sometimes it is very difficult to stand out in the crowd. Most of the time you'll feel better for keeping your principles, though there might be times when you will lose a friend, a job or some other situation. Christians are always called to stand on the side of righteousness even if it is unpopular to do so.

If you have trouble in withstanding the pressure to compromise, here are three principles that will help you through your day:

- Everyone you spend time with has an influence on you. Choose your friends wisely.
- Remember your uniqueness. You are special in God's eyes.
- Seek first the kingdom of God. Pleasing God is better than pleasing your friends.

Make Micah 6:8 a verse to live by:

He has showed you, O man, what is good. And what does the LORD require of you? To act justly and to love mercy and to walk humbly with your God.

GOING DEEPER

- After reading Romans 6:15-16, what loving advice would you have for someone who says to you, "I'm a Christian, so I can sin all I want because God will forgive me"?
- What areas in your life are vulnerable to compromise or taking advantage of the grace God has given you? Seek righteousness and be obedient to Jesus.

Further reading: John 8:34; 2 Peter 2:19.

The Secret of Endurance

In this you greatly rejoice, though now for a little while you may have had to suffer grief in all kinds of trials. These have come so that your faith—of greater worth than gold, which perishes even though refined by fire—may be proved genuine and may result in praise, glory and honor when Jesus Christ is revealed.

1 PETER 1:6-7

There is no doubt that you will experience trials in your Christian life. Some new Christians mistakenly believe that being a Christian means living a life free of hassles and struggles. God never promised us freedom from trials; He promised us that He would walk with us through the trials and help us to endure our hardships. No one looks forward to trials, but trials can produce a stronger faith. You can withstand anything that comes if you remember that every trial is actually a test. Before gold is pure it must be tested in the fire. The trials which come your way will test your faith, and out of your struggles your faith can emerge stronger than it ever was before.

The rigors which the athlete has to undergo are not meant to make him collapse but to help him develop strength and staying power. For the Christian, our trials are not meant to take the strength out of us, but to put the strength into us. Endurance through trials produces strength.

GOING DEEPER

- Reread 1 Peter 1:6-7. What effect do trials have on our faith?
- Are you experiencing trials right now in your life? You have a choice of how to deal with them: You can let them get you down, or you can see them as a way to test and strengthen your faith. How will you deal with your trials?

Further reading: Romans 5:2; 1 Peter 5:10; James 1:2; Job 23:10; Psalm 66:10; Proverbs 17:3.

You Are a Daily Gospel to the World

I have been crucified with Christ and I no longer live,
but Christ lives in me. The life I live in the body, I live by faith in
the Son of God, who loved me and gave himself for me.

GALATIANS 2:20

Your life is not your own; you were bought with a price—the high price and sacrifice of Jesus on the cross at Calvary. Although you may look the same and even have the same personality and mannerisms, on the inside you become a new person when Jesus Christ enters your life. You become a representative of your Lord wherever you go.

A little poem has always helped me understand that my new life in Christ is a daily gospel to the world. I am saying, as Paul said, "I have been crucified with Christ and I no longer live, but Christ lives in me. The life I live in the body, I live by faith in the Son of God, who loved me and gave himself for me."

Here's the poem:

You are writing a gospel,
A chapter each day,
By deeds that you do,
By words that you say.
Men read what you write,

Whether faithless or true,
Say, what is the gospel according to you?[1]

GOING DEEPER

- After reading Galatians 2:20, do you believe that Christ actually lives in you?
- If someone looked at your life, would they see a gospel of goodness and hope?

Further reading: Romans 6:6; 8:37; 1 Peter 4:2; Galatians 1:4.

Your Best Interest Is His Best Interest

He called the crowd to him along with his disciples and said, "If anyone would come after me, he must deny himself and take up his cross and follow me."

MARK 8:34

I recently read of a man who bought a hotel in Spokane, Washington. There was only one problem: The hotel's restaurant was the big moneymaker, since the bar grossed $10,000 a month. But the new owner wasn't going to keep the bar. It's not that he wanted to impose his own views on other people, but as a Christian he chose not to run a business subsidized by alcohol sales. The hotel manager argued with the new owner that if guests couldn't drink they would be out the door to a competitor. He also gave the new owner some convincing statistics showing that he couldn't make it financially without the bar. The owner listened politely and closed the door to the bar. He had to stick to his convictions. The manager promptly quit.

The owner remodeled the hotel lobby and turned the bar into a cozy coffee shop. In the first couple of years of business, food sales went up 20 percent and room bookings went up 30 percent. Still, profits weren't what they could have been if the bar were open.

But the hotel owner's reply was, "Beliefs aren't worth much if a fella's not ready to live by them!"

GOING DEEPER

- What risks are you willing to take to follow your beliefs?
- Are you willing to deny yourself in order to follow the call of Jesus? Don't let anyone kid you—there is a sense of self-denial when you get serious about getting in touch with God.

Further reading: Matthew 10:38; Luke 14:27.

Obedience

Sometimes It Isn't Easy

Love one another with brotherly affection; outdo one another in showing honor.

ROMANS 12:10, *RSV*

No one ever said that living the Christian life would be easy. The following words help give us perspective.

IT IS NOT EASY

to apologize
to begin over
to take advice
to be unselfish
to admit error
to face a sneer
to be charitable
to keep trying
to be considerate
to avoid mistakes
to endure success
to profit by mistakes
to forgive and forget
to think and then act
to keep out of a rut
to make the best of little
to subdue an unruly temper

to shoulder a deserved blame.
BUT IT ALWAYS PAYS.[1]

GOING DEEPER

- What makes it difficult for you to live out Romans 12:10 in your life? Which item on the list found in today's thought is most difficult for you to do?
- What would be the payoff if you did live out Romans 12:10 today?

Further reading: Hebrews 13:1; Philippians 2:3.

Slow Me Down, Lord

*Seek first his kingdom and his righteousness, and all these things will be
given to you as well. Therefore do not worry about tomorrow, for tomorrow
will worry about itself. Each day has enough trouble of its own.*

MATTHEW 6:33-34

We live in a fast-paced society where at times we can become
seduced by a culture that gets our mind off the Lord. To keep in
touch with Jesus we must slow down our fierce pace and give Jesus
our time and attention. This prayer has helped me for years with my
tendency to overcommit my life to unimportant things and leave
God on the sideline.

Slow Me Down, Lord

Ease the pounding of my heart by the quieting of my
    mind.
Steady my hurried pace with a vision of the eternal reach
    of time.
Give me, amid the confusion of the day, the calmness of
    the everlasting hills.
Break the tensions of my nerves and muscles with the
    soothing music of the singing streams that live in my
    memory.
Teach me the art of taking minute vacations—of slowing
    down to look at a flower, to chat with a friend, to pat

a dog, to smile at a child, to read a few lines from a good book.

Slow me down, Lord, and inspire me to send my roots deep into the soil of life's enduring values, that I may grow toward my greater destiny.

Remind me each day that the race is not always to the swift; that there is more to life than increasing its speed.

Let me look upward to the towering oak and know that it grew great and strong because it grew slowly and well.[1]

GOING DEEPER

- After reading Matthew 6:33-34, what does the Bible suggest be our first priority?
- Are your priorities in proper perspective? Take a few minutes to give God your priorities and seek His kingdom first.

Further reading: Psalm 37:4; Proverbs 3:5-6.

A Hunger for Holiness

As obedient children, do not conform to the evil desires you had when
you lived in ignorance. But just as he who called you is holy, so be holy in all
you do; for it is written: "Be holy, because I am holy."

1 P E T E R   1 : 1 4 - 1 6

Every Christian is called to live a life of holiness. I'm afraid I've been guilty of wanting spectacular results in my Christian life but giving only a mediocre effort. Nobel prizewinner Mother Teresa put it best when she said, "Our progress in holiness depends on God and our-selves—on God's grace and on our will to be holy." Pray today for a hunger for holiness. Holiness, or to be holy, means to be set apart or kept pure. Holiness is the everyday business of every Christian. It evidences itself in the decisions we make and the lifestyle we live, hour by hour, day by day. Andrew Murray said, "The starting point and the goal of our Christian life is obedience." Through obedience to God and His Word your life will become more holy. The goal to live a life of holiness is a lifelong process of sanctification and spir-itual maturity. Some people never strive to become mature believ-ers. The first step of holiness is a willingness to be obedient. The result of holiness is a fuller and deeper life with God. Jesus put it this way: "Blessed are those who hunger and thirst for righteous-ness, for they will be filled" (Matt. 5:6).

GOING DEEPER

- What challenge does 1 Peter 1:14-16 give you as a Christian?
- Do you have a hunger for holiness? God's desire is for you to be holy as He is holy. He'll do His part; will you do yours?

Further reading: Romans 12:2; 2 Corinthians 7:1; 1 Thessalonians 4:7; Leviticus 11:44-45.

Trust or Worry?

I tell you, do not worry about your life, what you will eat or drink;
or about your body, what you will wear. Is not life more important than
food, and the body more important than clothes?

MATTHEW 6:25

Did you know that some psychologists claim that 85 percent of what we worry about will never happen to us? They say there is absolutely nothing we can do about the next 10 percent of our worries, and that only the other 5 percent of our worries are legitimate. When you take a look at your worries in the light of these statistics, wouldn't you agree that most of your worrying is useless?

There are more people in hospital beds because of worry than almost any other disease. Headaches, ulcers, heart attacks, mental disorders and even the common cold can be brought on by worry.

Worry is the opposite of trust, and as a Christian you are called to put your trust in God's direction for your life. One of the greatest pieces of advice ever given to humankind is from the Sermon on the Mount when Jesus said:

Therefore I tell you, do not worry about your life, what you will eat or drink; or about your body, what you will wear. Is not life more important than food, and the body more important than clothes? Look at the birds of the air; they do not sow or reap or store away in barns, and yet your heavenly Father feeds them. Are you not much more valuable than they? Who of you by worrying can add a single hour to his life?

And why do you worry about clothes? See how the lilies of the field grow. They do not labor or spin. Yet I tell you that not even Solomon in all his splendor was dressed like one of these. If that is how God clothes the grass of the field, which is here today and tomorrow is thrown into the fire, will he not much more clothe you, O you of little faith? So do not worry, saying, "What shall we eat?" or "What shall we drink?" or "What shall we wear?" For the pagans run after all these things, and your heavenly Father knows that you need them. But seek first his kingdom and his righteousness, and all these things will be given to you as well (Matt. 6:25-33).

The decision to trust God or to carry the worries of the world yourself is up to you. Either road you decide to take requires an action decision on your part. One road leads to fulfillment and peace—the other road leads to frustration and anxiety. By all means choose the road called trust! God's Word has never been proven wrong.

GOING DEEPER

- If Jesus tells us in Matthew 6:25 not to worry about basic needs like food, water and clothing, what do you think He would suggest about the things you are worrying about right now?
- Do you struggle with worry and anxiety? If you do, then make a conscious decision to place your trust and faith in the Creator of our universe, who sees beyond what our finite self can see.

Further reading: Luke 10:4; Philippians 4:6; 1 Peter 5:7.

Goals for Daily Living

In his heart a man plans his course, but the LORD determines his steps.

PROVERBS 16:9

Have you ever written down goals for living your life? I'm not talking about the dos and don'ts of legalism. I mean forming a philosophy of life and then living your life to the fullest according to your goals.

F. B. Meyer was a great writer and minister of the gospel. He had seven goals for daily living that I use and recommend:

1. Make a daily, definite consecration of yourself to God (audibly).
2. Tell God you are willing to be willing about all.
3. Reckon on Christ to do His part perfectly.
4. Confess sin instantly.
5. Hand over to Christ every temptation and care.
6. Keep in touch with Christ. (Read the Word and good books; pray; seek places and people where He is.)
7. Expect the Holy Spirit to work in, with and for you.[1]

GOING DEEPER

- Write Proverbs 16:9 on an index card and put it somewhere where you will see it often. Better yet, memorize it!

- What are the goals you live by? Today write out some goals, or take on F. B. Meyer's goals and pledge yourself to living by them each and every day.

Further reading: Jeremiah 10:23.

Walking in the Light

This is the message we have heard from him and declare to you:
God is light; in him there is no darkness at all. If we claim to have fellowship
with him yet walk in the darkness, we lie and do not live by the truth.
But if we walk in the light, as he is in the light, we have fellowship with one
another, and the blood of Jesus, his Son, purifies us from all sin.

1 JOHN 1:5-7

Jesus said, "I am the light of the world. Whoever follows me will never walk in darkness, but will have the light of life" (John 8:12). The concept of light is an important concept throughout the Bible. When you walk with Jesus, you walk in the light. Light helps you to see where you are going. Without the light of God you cannot possibly know how to live your life. Living in darkness is incompatible with living in the light. If you want to walk with God, you've got to stay away from the darkness and walk in the light.

In today's Scripture there are two important results of walking in the light. The first result is fellowship with one another—in other words, a right relationship with our family and friends. Secondly, when we walk in the light the blood of Jesus purifies or cleanses us from all sin, restoring a right relationship with God. When we walk in the light we have a right relationship horizontally with humankind and a right relationship vertically with God. There are no more important priorities in life.

It is interesting to note that many studies in the area of death and dying tell us that just before a person dies he seeks a right relationship with God and a right relationship with his family and friends. When all other aspects of life are put aside, the important priorities of life remain. The way to insure that your life is in proper perspective is to walk in the light.

GOING DEEPER

- Reread 1 John 1:5-7. What attribute of God is described in these verses? What are the two results of walking in the light?
- Are there areas of darkness in your life? If so, how about shedding some light on them and giving them over to Christ? God's light will enable you to see where you should going!

Further reading: 1 John 3:11; 2 Corinthians 6:14; John 3:19-21; Hebrews 9:14.

His Way or Your Way?

Jesus answered, "I am the way and the truth and the life. No one comes to the Father except through me."

JOHN 14:6

He is the Way. Follow Him through the Land of Unlikeness; You will see rare beasts, and have unique adventures.

He is the Truth. See Him in the Kingdom of Anxiety; You will come to a great city that has expected your return for years.

He is the Life. Love Him in the World of the Flesh; And at your marriage all of its occasions shall dance for joy.[1]

When we read the words of Jesus, "I am the way and the truth and the life," sometimes we forget that He has become our substance of life. When You follow and accept His way, truth and life, He will bring you to places and experiences beyond the normal human life. When your life is in His hands, following His call, you are on the greatest adventure that life has to offer. Nobody said it will be easy, but you can't deny that His calling in your life is the right one. Go for it—and keep your eyes fixed on Jesus so you don't lose your way!

Going Deeper

- In the Bible passage John 14:6, what three ways does Jesus describe Himself? Underline the word "the" every time it occurs in the verse. Why is this little word so important?
- What will it take for you to follow His way, obey His truth and live His life?

Further reading: John 10:9; John 11:25.

Jesus Is Lord

The Uniqueness of Christ

Jesus answered, "I am the way and the truth and the life.
No one comes to the Father except through me."

JOHN 14:6

No person who has ever walked this earth even comes close in comparison with Jesus Christ. He is unique. He is incomparable. He is our Lord. Here is what one unknown person wrote about Him years ago:

> More than 1900 years ago there was a Man born contrary to the laws of life. This Man lived in poverty and was reared in obscurity. He did not travel extensively. Only once did He cross the boundary of the country in which He lived; that was during His exile in childhood. He possessed neither wealth nor influence. His relatives were inconspicuous and had neither training nor formal education.

> In infancy He startled a king; in childhood He puzzled doctors; in manhood He ruled the course of nature, walked upon the billows as if pavement and hushed the sea to sleep. He healed the multitudes without medicine and made no charge for His service.

> He never wrote a book, yet all the libraries of the country could not hold the books that have been written about Him.

He never wrote a song, and yet He has furnished the theme for more songs than all the songwriters combined. He never founded a college, but all the schools put together cannot boast of having as many students. He never marshaled an army, nor drafted a soldier, nor fired a gun; and yet no leader ever had more volunteers who have, under His orders, made more rebels stack arms and surrender without a shot fired. He never practiced medicine, and yet He has healed more broken hearts than all the doctors far and near.

Every seventh day the wheels of commerce cease their turning as multitudes wend their way to worshiping assemblies to pay homage and respect to Him. The names of the past proud statesmen of Greece and Rome have come and gone, but the name of this Man abounds more and more. Though time has spread 1900 years between the people of this generation and the scene of His crucifixion, yet He still lives. Herod could not destroy Him, and the grave could not hold Him.

He stands forth upon the highest pinnacle of heavenly glory, proclaimed of God, acknowledged by angels, adored by saints, and feared by devils as the living, personal Christ, our Lord and Savior.[1]

GOING DEEPER

- What does John 14:6 tells us about Jesus Christ?
- What four gifts can a relationship with Jesus Christ offer you?

Further reading: John 10:9; John 11:25; John 1:4.

Open Your Heart to Jesus

Here I am! I stand at the door and knock. If anyone hears my voice and opens the door, I will come in and eat with him, and he with me.

REVELATION 3:20

Billy Graham once said;

> I have searched the world over in my travels for contented and happy men. I have found such men only where Christ has been personally and decisively received. There is only one permanent way to have peace of soul that wells up in joy, contentment and happiness, and that is by repentance of sin and personal faith in Jesus Christ as Savior.[1]

Throughout the centuries Jesus Christ continues to heal broken hearts and broken spirits. All over the world today He is placing hope into shattered lives and peace into troubled souls. When you get in touch with Jesus Christ, one thing is guaranteed: You will never remain the same. I love the old Russian proverb that says, "He who has this disease called Jesus Christ will never be cured."

GOING DEEPER

- Revelation 3:20 tells us that Jesus is standing at the door of our hearts. What must we do before He can come into our hearts?

- What do you think the meaning of the phrase, "I will come in and eat with him, and he with me," in Revelation 3:20 might be?

Further reading: Matthew 24:33; Luke 12:36; John 14:23.

The Resurrection of Jesus Christ

If Christ has not been raised, your faith is futile; you are still in your sins.

1 C O R I N T H I A N S 1 5 : 1 7

The resurrection of Jesus Christ from the dead is the cornerstone of our Christian faith. If Christ did not rise from the dead, your faith is in vain. But you can be assured that the good news is true. Jesus Christ "was buried [and] he was raised on the third day according to the Scriptures" (1 Cor. 15:4).

Throughout the ages skeptics have tried to disprove the Resurrection experience, but it stands the test of time. Here are six proofs that Jesus actually rose from the dead:

First Proof—The Resurrection was foretold by Jesus Christ, the Son of God.

> From that time on Jesus began to explain to his disciples that he must go to Jerusalem and suffer many things at the hands of the elders, chief priests and teachers of the law, and that he must be killed and on the third day be raised to life (Matt. 16:21).

Second Proof—The Resurrection is the only reasonable explanation for His empty tomb.

> Joseph bought some linen cloth, took down the body, wrapped it in the linen, and placed it in a tomb cut out of

rock. Then he rolled a stone against the entrance of the tomb (Mark 15:46).

Third Proof—The Resurrection is the only reasonable explanation for the appearance of Jesus Christ to His disciples.

> He was buried . . . raised on the third day according to the Scriptures, and . . . appeared to Peter, and then to the Twelve. After that, he appeared to more than five hundred of the brothers at the same time, most of whom are still living, though some have fallen asleep. Then he appeared to . . . me also, as to one abnormally born (1 Cor. 15:4-8).

Fourth Proof—The Resurrection is the only reasonable explanation for the beginning of the Christian Church.

> This man was handed over to you by God's set purpose and foreknowledge; and you, with the help of wicked men, put him to death by nailing him to the cross. But God raised him from the dead, freeing him from the agony of death, because it was impossible for death to keep its hold on him (Acts 2:23-24).

Fifth Proof—The Resurrection is the only reasonable explanation for the transformation of the disciples.

> The disciples went into hiding in an upper room "for fear of the Jews" (John 20:19). After seeing and talking with Jesus for approximately six weeks, they went out to "turn the world upside down" (see Acts 17:6), fearlessly proclaiming Jesus Christ (also see Acts 3:12-26; 4:1-33; 8:4; 17:6).

Sixth Proof—The witness of the apostle Paul, and the transformation of his life, can be reasonably explained only because of the resurrection of Christ.

> Saul grew more and more powerful and baffled the Jews living in Damascus by proving that Jesus is the Christ (Acts 9:22).

GOING DEEPER

- Reread 1 Corinthians 15:17. Why is it important that Jesus rose from the dead?
- Why are these six proofs important to your faith and life?

Further reading: Romans 4:25; Romans 5:6-8; Isaiah 53:5-6.

The Incarnation

The Word became flesh and made his dwelling among us.
We have seen his glory, the glory of the One and Only, who came
from the Father, full of grace and truth.

JOHN 1:14

How do you package love? God used a stable and straw on the eve of Christ's birth. The Incarnation means that Jesus Christ is God in the flesh. Paul put it this way, "He is the image of the invisible God" (Col. 1:15, *NKJV*).

I heard a story as a child that helped me understand this concept. It's about ants.

> Once upon a time there was a colony of ants who were busy doing whatever ants do with their lives. God wanted to tell the ants of His love for them and His eternal home prepared for them. What was the very best way for God to communicate to those ants? The only possible way to speak to the ants was to become an ant and speak their language. So He did, and they believed.

The only way for us to fully recognize God was for God to come to Earth in the form of a man to identify with the world. Jesus was fully God and fully and completely identified with humankind. Hebrews 2:17-18 helps us understand the incarnation of Jesus and how He relates to our life:

For this reason he had to be made like his brothers in every way, in order that he might become a merciful and faithful high priest in service to God, and that he might make atonement for the sins of the people. Because he himself suffered when he was tempted, he is able to help those who are being tempted.

GOING DEEPER

- John 1:14 tells us that the Word became flesh and lived for a while among us. Who or what is the Word, and why is this Scripture so important?
- How does it make you feel to know that God loves you so much that He went out of His way to connect with you?

Further reading: Galatians 4:4; Philippians 2:7-8; 1 Timothy 3:16; Hebrews 2:14.

Jesus Is Lord

Let all Israel be assured of this: God has made this Jesus,
whom you crucified, both Lord and Christ.

A C T S   2 : 3 6

In the Gospels there is a graphic story of Jesus standing before Pontius Pilate, the Roman governor. At one point in the story Pilate offers to release a prisoner to the Jews. He offers either Jesus or Barabbas (who was a troublemaker and murderer). The crowd asks for Barabbas to be freed. Pilate doesn't know what to do. He asks the crowd, "What shall I do with the man Jesus?" They cry, "Crucify him!"

The question Pilate asked is still the important question of the day. When people today are confronted with Christ, they basically have four options. Which option have you chosen?

1. *Reject Him*—Turn your back on Jesus and live your life without Him.
2. *Ignore Him*—Choose to be an Easter and Christmas Christian. Acknowledge His deity but keep Him out of the practical daily activities of your life.
3. *Appease Him*—There are the people who go through the motions of Christianity but still keep the lordship of Christ at a distance.
4. *Obey Him*—If you obey Him, you are choosing to make Him Lord of your life. You are no longer in control, He is. You choose to obey His will and His Word.

What will you do with the claims of Christ in your life? If you fall into one of the categories besides obedience, then perhaps it's time to make Him the Lord of your life. If you believe He is Christ the Savior, then your only true option is to make Him Christ the Lord also!

GOING DEEPER

- What does Acts 2:36 tell us about what God made Jesus to be?
- Assuming that Jesus is Lord (and He is), what will you do with Jesus Christ? Of the four possible options above, which option have you chosen?
- If you believe that Jesus is your Savior, then the next step is to make Him your Lord and give Him control of your life.

Further reading: Luke 2:11.

Lord, Liar or Lunatic?

I and the Father are one.

JOHN 10:30

On a recent airplane trip a woman saw me reading the Bible. She was curious and asked me point-blank if I really believed that Jesus Christ was the Son of God. I replied that I indeed believed that Jesus is the Christ, the Son of the living God. Then she asked, "Isn't it difficult for you to intellectually believe such a preposterous statement as Jesus being God's only Son?"

My reply went something like this: "In the Bible, Jesus claimed to be the Messiah, the Son of God. Since Jesus claimed equality with God, that leaves me with only three options. He was either a liar, a lunatic or the Lord who He claimed to be." Well, she didn't like any of those options. She said she believed Him to be "a great teacher of faith in God, but not equal to God." But I replied, "He didn't leave that option open for us. He said He was equal with God. He either lied about that statement, and was deceitful, or He actually believed He was God but was crazy, or else He really was God. There are no other options."

I'm not sure we got a convert that day, but she was doing some serious thinking.

I like what C. S. Lewis writes about this subject: "I am trying here to prevent anyone saying the really foolish thing that people often say about Him: 'I'm ready to accept Jesus as a great moral teacher, but I don't accept His claim to be God.' That is the one thing we must not say. A man who was merely a man and said the sort of things Jesus said would not be a great moral teacher. He would either be a lunatic—on a level with the man who says he is a poached egg—or else he would be the Devil of Hell. You must make your choice. Either this man was, and is, the Son of God, or else a madman or something worse."

Then Lewis adds, "You can shut Him up for a fool, you can spit at Him and kill Him as a demon; or you can fall at His feet and call Him Lord and God. But let us not come up with any patronizing nonsense about His being a great human teacher. He has not left that open to us. He did not intend to."[1]

GOING DEEPER

- John 10:30 states that Jesus and the Father are one. Do you find this statement difficult to believe? Why or why not?
- Today, are you living as if Jesus is the Lord of your life?

Further reading: John 17:21-23.

The Influence of One Life

God exalted him to the highest place and gave him the name
that is above every name, that at the name of Jesus every knee should bow,
in heaven and on earth and under the earth, and every tongue confess that
Jesus Christ is Lord, to the glory of God the Father.

PHILIPPIANS 2:9-11

Today millions and millions of people worship Jesus Christ. Their language may be different from yours, and even their approach to worship will vary in every culture and denomination. But when all is said and done, the influence of our Lord Jesus Christ has affected life on this earth more than that of all other men or religions combined. Today in every part of the world people kneel before Him; like you and I, they stand amazed at His influence in our world. These beautiful words help us understand the powerful influence of this one life.

Here is a man who was born in an obscure village, the child of a peasant woman. He grew up in another village. He worked in a carpenter shop until He was 30, and then for three years He was an itinerant preacher. He never wrote a book. He never held office. He never owned a home. He never had a family. He never went to college. He never put His feet inside a big city. He never traveled more than 200 miles from the place where He was born. He never did one of the things that usually accompany greatness. He had no credentials but Himself.

While still a young man, the tide of popular opinion turned against Him. His friends ran away. One of them denied Him. He was turned over to His enemies. He went through the mockery of a trial. He was nailed upon a cross between two thieves. While He was dying His executioners gambled for the only piece of property He had on earth, and that was His coat. When He was dead He was taken down and laid in a borrowed grave through the pity of a friend.

Nineteen wide centuries have come and gone, and today He is the centerpiece of the human race and the leader of the column of progress.

I am far within the mark when I say that all the armies that ever marched, and all the names that were ever built, and all the parliaments that ever sat, and all the kings that ever reigned, put together have not affected the life of man upon this earth as has that one solitary life.[1]

GOING DEEPER

- Take a few moments to pause and reflect on the impact Jesus Christ has had on the world around you. What do you think the world would be like if Jesus Christ wasn't Lord?
- Have you bowed before the throne of God and confessed with your tongue that Jesus Christ is Lord?

Further reading: Philippians 2:9-11.

Commitment

Radical Commitment

Jesus replied: "'Love the Lord your God with all your heart and with all your soul and with all your mind.' This is the first and greatest commandment. And the second is like it: 'Love your neighbor as yourself.' All the Law and the Prophets hang on these two commandments."

MATTHEW 22:37-40

Our love for God goes beyond lip service or sitting in the pew on Sunday. God wants all that we have and all that we are to become His. Sometimes the actions of people of other faiths or causes put my actions to shame. The following letter was written by a communist student who broke off his engagement with his fiancée. While you read this letter, think how it compares to your commitment and dedication to Jesus Christ.

> We communists have a high casualty rate. We are the ones who get shot and hung and ridiculed and fired from our jobs and in every other way made as uncomfortable as possible. A certain percentage of us get killed or imprisoned. We live in virtual poverty. We turn back to the party every penny we make above what is absolutely necessary to keep us alive. We communists do not have the time or the money for many movies, or concerts, or T-bone steaks, or decent homes, or new cars. We have been described as fanatics. We are fanatics. Our lives are dominated by one great overshadowing factor: the struggle for world communism. We communists have a

philosophy of life which no amount of money can buy. We have a cause to fight for, a definite purpose in life. We subordinate our petty personal selves into the great movement of humanity; and if our personal lives seem hard or our egos appear to suffer through subordination to the party, then we are adequately compensated by the thought that each of us in his small way is contributing to something new and true and better for mankind. There is one thing in which I am dead earnest about, and that is the communist cause. It is my life, my business, my religion, my hobby, my sweetheart, my wife, and my mistress, my breath and meat. I work at it in the daytime and dream of it at night. Its hold on me grows, not lessens, as time goes on; therefore, I cannot carry on a friendship, a love affair, or even a conversation without relating it to this force which both drives and guides my life. I evaluate people, books, ideas, and actions according to how they affect the communist cause, and by their attitude toward it. I've already been in jail because of my ideals, and if necessary, I'm ready to go before a firing squad.[1]

GOING DEEPER

- What two important commandments are given in Matthew 22:37-40? What parts of your life do these commandments directly apply too?
- Can you speak similar words about your commitment to Jesus as the communist student did about his faith in the communist cause? What does it mean for you to love God with your whole heart, mind and soul?

Further reading: Deuteronomy 6:5; Leviticus 19:18; Matthew 5:43-44; Galatians 5:14.

Full Surrender

I urge you, brothers, in view of God's mercy, to offer your bodies as living sacrifices, holy and pleasing to God—this is your spiritual act of worship. Do not conform any longer to the pattern of this world, but be transformed by the renewing of your mind. Then you will be able to test and approve what God's will is—his good, pleasing and perfect will.

ROMANS 12:1-2

What are practical ways you can fully surrender your life to God? Sometimes we get too comfortable in our lifestyle. Here's a gentle reminder.

I would love to buy $3 worth of God, please, not enough to explode my soul or disturb my sleep, but just enough to equal a cup of warm milk or a snooze in the sunshine. I don't want enough of Him to make me love a black man or pick beets with a migrant. I want ecstasy, not transformation; I want the warmth of the womb, not a new birth. I want a pound of the Eternal in a paper sack. I would like to buy $3 worth of God, please.[1]

I'm afraid too many people approach their Christian faith as if they wanted to buy three dollars' worth of God. They want only the best that God has to offer. As today's Scripture points out, you can't have both. God's desire for your life is that you actually give your body as a living sacrifice to Him. If you choose to identify with Jesus, you are choosing to make Him the Master of your life. A life fully surrendered to Jesus is lived on the edge of adventure.

GOING DEEPER

- Romans 12:1-2 challenges us to give our bodies as living sacrifices. How would you define a living sacrifice?
- Are there certain areas of your life that you have yet to surrender to God? Maybe it's your finances or a personal relationship or even an area of your spiritual discipline. Is now the time to give it all to Jesus?

Further reading: Ephesians 4:1; Romans 6:13-16; 1 Peter 2:5.

Overcommitment and Fatigue: A Deadly Sin

They who wait for the LORD shall renew their strength,
they shall mount up with wings like eagles, they shall run and not
be weary, they shall walk and not faint.

ISAIAH 40:31, RSV

We live in a culture that has often fooled us into believing that more is better and busyness is a virtue. Far too many people in our world are spiritually, emotionally and physically bankrupt because they are overcommitted and fatigued. Vince Lombardi said, "Fatigue makes cowards of us all." The comedian Flip Wilson summed it up best for many of us when he said, "If I had my entire life to live over again, I doubt if I'd have the strength."

I don't believe that God wants us to be one step from a nervous breakdown, always on the edge of exhaustion. What's the answer? There are no easy formulas for success, but there are two suggestions I want you to think about today.

1. *Cut back and do less.* If this means making less money, cutting back on your social obligations or even taking a night off from church activities, do whatever it takes to not be so overcommitted and fatigued. A friend of mine once told me, "If the devil can't make you bad, he'll make you busy."

2. *Rest.* Rest should be a nonnegotiable time in everyone's life. Even God rested! Exodus 31:17 (*RSV*) says, "In six days the LORD made heaven and earth, and on the seventh day he rested, and was refreshed." When we rest we get a proper perspective on our life. When we rest we can reflect on what has taken place in our life during the week. Does your life have control of you, or do you have control of your life? Rest and reflection will help you answer that important question.

GOING DEEPER

- What does it mean to "wait for the Lord," as written in Isaiah 40:31? What does this verse tell us is the result of waiting for the Lord?
- Today take an evaluation of your fatigue and overcommitment level. If you are spiritually, emotionally or physically bankrupt, then it's time to cut back, do less and rest. What is the next day you have scheduled to relax?

Further reading: Luke 18:1; 2 Corinthians 4:16; Psalm 103:5; 2 Corinthians 4:1; Hebrews 12:1-3.

Try It ... You'll Like It!

Taste and see that the LORD is good; blessed is the man who takes refuge in him.

PSALM 34:8

One of my favorite storytellers is Dr. Anthony Campolo. I love how he tells the story of Blondin, the tightrope-walker who in the 1890s strung a tightrope across Niagara Falls.

> Before ten thousand screaming people [he] inched his way from the Canadian side of the falls to the United States side. When he got there the crowd began shouting his name: "Blondin! Blondin! Blondin! Blondin!"
>
> Finally he raised his arms, quieted the crowd, and [how's this for an ego trip?] shouted to them, "I am Blondin! Do you believe in me?" The crowd shouted back, "We believe! We believe! We believe!"
>
> Again he quieted the crowd, and once more he shouted to them, "I'm going back across the tightrope, but this time I'm going to carry someone on my back. Do you believe I can do that?" The crowd yelled, "We believe! We believe!"
>
> He quieted them one more time, and then he said, "Who will be that person?" The crowd went dead. Nothing.
>
> Finally, out of the crowd stepped one man. He climbed on Blondin's shoulders, and for the next three-and-a-half hours, Blondin inched his way back across the tightrope to the Canadian side of the falls.

The point of the story is blatantly clear: Ten thousand people stood there that day chanting, "We believe, we believe!" But only one person really believed. Believing is not just saying, "I accept the fact." Believing is giving your life over into the hands of the one in whom you say you believe.[1]

Christ calls you to step out of your comfort zone and walk with Him. Stepping out on faith means that you don't know all that is going to happen but you are putting your trust in Someone who does. Putting your trust in Jesus is not always the comfortable way to go. The risk you take is that God knows what He is doing better than you know what you are doing. History and common sense tell me to put my faith in the infinite Creator and Savior of the universe rather than in unstable me. Are you ready to take another step in the direction of faith? Then accept God's challenge to taste and see.

GOING DEEPER

- Psalm 34:8 tells us that we must take action and make the effort to find out how good the Lord is. Have you ever truly taken refuge in Him?
- What are you doing right now in your life that could not be done without the supernatural power of Christ? Those who live their lives in touch with Jesus are not afraid to step out of their comfort zone and into the realm of faith.

Further reading: 1 Peter 2:3; Psalm 2:12.

We Are an Offering

Commit your way to the LORD; trust in him, and he will act.

PSALM 37:5, RSV

On many a Sunday morning at our church we sing a song titled "We Are An Offering." It deeply expresses my desire to be God's person. Here is what the song says:

We lift our voices, we lift our hands;
We lift our lives up to You, we are an offering.
Lord, use our voices, Lord, use our hands,
Lord, use our lives—they are Yours, we are an offering.
All that we are, all that we have,
All that we hope to be we give to You, we give to You.[1]

Paul challenged the Christians in Rome, "In view of God's mercy . . . offer your bodies as living sacrifices, holy and pleasing to God—this is your spiritual act of worship" (Rom. 12:1). Jesus was an offering on the cross for our salvation. Our lives in return must be a living offering to our Lord and Savior Jesus Christ.

GOING DEEPER

- God promises that He will be active in our lives. What two steps, found in Psalm 37:5, must we take to claim that promise?

- Do you view your life as an offering to God? Today pray the prayer in the song above: "Lord, use my voice; Lord, use my hands; Lord, use my life."

Further reading: Psalm 4:5; 55:22; Proverbs 16:3.

No More Excuses

Some time later, Jesus went up to Jerusalem for a feast of the Jews.
Now there is in Jerusalem near the Sheep Gate a pool, which in Aramaic is
called Bethesda and which is surrounded by five covered colonnades.
Here a great number of disabled people used to lie—the blind, the lame,
the paralyzed. One who was there had been an invalid for thirty-eight years.
When Jesus saw him lying there and learned that he had been in this condition
for a long time, he asked him, "Do you want to get well?"

"Sir," the invalid replied, "I have no one to help me into the pool
when the water is stirred. While I am trying to get in, someone else
goes down ahead of me."

Then Jesus said to him, "Get up! Pick up your mat and walk."

JOHN 5:1-8

I'm convinced that procrastination should be added to the seven deadly sins in the book of Proverbs. There is a great tendency among us human beings to put off making commitments and living life to the fullest. The excuses are abysmal: "When I get out of school, then I'll commit my life to God"; "When I get married, then my life will be happy"; "As soon as I have some money, my life will change."

In today's Scripture we meet a man who had been crippled for 38 years. Jesus asked him the big question: "Do you want to get well?" Notice that he didn't answer the question with an immediate yes, but hesitated and made an excuse. At times we are so much like the sick man: We know what God wants us to do, but we pause and make an excuse.

One morning a vulture was hungry. While flying over the river, he saw a dead animal's carcass floating down the river on a piece of ice. The vulture landed on the ice and began to gorge himself with this delightful meal. He looked up to take a breath of air and noticed that he was 100 yards from a waterfall and that the ice was moving rapidly toward the waterfall. But instead of flying away, he kept eating, though keeping his eye on the waterfall. At 25 yards he decided to take one last bite. Then at 10 yards he took one last mouthful. With only a few feet to go before the falls he tried to fly, but his feet were now frozen to the ice, and he tumbled to his death over the falls.[1]

Don't make excuses! Many a person has wasted his life by putting off the vital long-term priorities for the less important short-term ones.

GOING DEEPER

- The man in today's Scripture passage was sitting in one spot for 38 years. What could he have done to get to the pool instead of sitting there?
- Is there something in your life that you have been putting off with a feeble excuse? Make a commitment now!

Further reading: Matthew 9:5-6; Mark. 2:11; Luke 5:24.

Taking a Stand

The man who loves his life will lose it, while the man who hates his life
in this world will keep it for eternal life. Whoever serves me must follow me;
and where I am, my servant also will be. My Father will honor
the one who serves me.

J O H N   1 2 : 2 5 - 2 6

Today's story shows how one insignificant person can make a difference in the history of the world. All it takes is faith and a single-
minded belief that you are one of Christ's healing agents to a
lonely and hurting world.

In the fourth century there lived an Asiatic monk who had
spent most of his life in a remote prayer community, rais-
ing vegetables for the cloister kitchen. When he was not
tending his garden spot, he was fulfilling his vocation of
study and prayer.

Then one day this monk, named Telemachus, felt that
the Lord wanted him to go to Rome, the capital of the
world—the busiest, wealthiest, biggest city in the world.
Telemachus had no idea why he should go there, and he
was terrified at the thought. But as he prayed, God's direc-
tive became clear.

How bewildered the little monk must have been as he
set out on the long journey, on foot, over dusty roads west-
ward, everything he owned on his back! Why was he going?
He didn't know. What would he find there? He had no idea.
But obediently, he went.

Telemachus arrived in Rome during the holiday festival. You may know that the Roman rulers kept the ghettos quiet in those days by providing free bread and special entertainment called circuses. At the time Telemachus arrived the city was also bustling with excitement over the recent Roman victory over the Goths. In the midst of this jubilant commotion, the monk looked for clues as to why God had brought him there, for he had no guidance, not even a superior in a religious order to contact.

Perhaps, he thought, it is not sheer coincidence that I have arrived at this festival time. Perhaps God has some special role for me to play.

So Telemachus let the crowds guide him, and the stream of humanity soon led him into the Coliseum, where the gladiator contests were to be staged. He could hear the cries of the animals in their caves beneath the floor of the great arena and the clamor of the contestants preparing to do battle.

The gladiators marched into the arena, saluted the emperor, and shouted, "We who are about to die salute thee." Telemachus shuddered. He had never heard of gladiator games before, but had a premonition of awful violence.

The crowd had come to cheer men who, for no reason other than amusement, would murder each other. Human lives were offered for entertainment. As the monk realized what was going to happen, he realized he could not sit still and watch such savagery. Neither could he leave and forget. He jumped to the top of the perimeter wall and cried, "In the name of Christ, forbear!"

The fighting began, of course. No one paid the slightest heed to the puny voice. So Telemachus pattered down the stone steps and leapt onto the sandy floor of the arena. He made a comic figure—a scrawny man in a monk's habit dashing back and forth between muscular, armed athletes.

One gladiator sent him sprawling with a blow from his shield, directing him back to his seat. It was a rough gesture, though almost a kind one. The crowd roared.

But Telemachus refused to stop. He rushed into the way of those trying to fight, shouting again, "In the name of Christ, forbear!" The crowd began to laugh and cheer him on, perhaps thinking him part of the entertainment.

Then his movement blocked the vision of one of the contestants; the gladiator saw a blow coming just in time. Furious now, the crowd began to cry for the interloper's blood.

"Run him through!" they screamed.

The gladiator he had blocked raised his sword and with a flash of steel struck Telemachus, slashing down across his chest and into his stomach. The little monk gasped once more, "In the name of Christ, forbear."

Then a strange thing occurred. As the two gladiators and the crowd focused on the still form on the suddenly crimson sand, the arena fell deathly quiet. In the silence, someone in the top tier got up and walked out. Another followed. All over the arena, spectators began to leave, until the huge stadium was emptied.

There were other forces at work, of course, but that innocent figure lying in the pool of blood crystallized the opposition, and that was the last gladiatorial contest in the Roman Coliseum. Never again did men kill each other for the crowds' entertainment in the Roman arena.[1]

GOING DEEPER

- Reread John 12:25-26. What do we have to gain from following and serving Jesus Christ?

- Has God placed a cause worth fighting for in your life? Maybe it is time for you to take a stand on the side of justice.

Further reading: Matthew 10:39; Mark 8:35.

DAY 50

Accountability and Support

Therefore confess your sins to each other and pray for each other so that you may be healed. The prayer of a righteous man is powerful and effective.

JAMES 5:16

Who has access to your soul? Is there someone in your life with whom you can share anything and everything? Who keeps you accountable to living out your Christian faith with integrity? For many people who are trying to live the Christian life totally on their own, it comes with difficulty. We all need support. We all need people around us who can ask us the probing questions and encourage us to keep on moving in the right direction in our faith.

Notice that Scripture is full of examples of people needing and belonging to a community of believers who could encourage, support and exhort each other. When Moses was exhausted and drained, he had people actually come alongside him and hold up his staff to help win a battle over the Amalekites. Jesus chose 12 disciples to basically pour His life into for three years. He taught them to support each other. After Jesus rose from the dead the disciples in Jerusalem shared all things in common. They regularly ate, prayed and worshiped together (see Acts 2:42-47).

If you are in not in some type of accountability relationship or support group, then I challenge you to join a group. Or ask a friend to meet with you on a regular basis to share your faith journey with them. Here are a few questions to ask that can help you hold each other accountable and go deeper more quickly:

1. Have I been in a compromising situation with someone of the opposite sex this week?
2. Have I read or viewed anything that could be termed sexually explicit?
3. Have I given priority to my family this week?
4. Have I spent adequate time in Bible study and prayer this week?
5. Have I had any financial dealings that have lacked integrity?
6. Have I lied, cheated or harmed anyone with gossip this week?
7. Have I just lied to you on any of the above questions?

GOING DEEPER

- According to James 5:16, we are to be in such a close spiritual relationship with someone that we will confess our sins to each other. What makes this so difficult to do?
- We all need an accountability and support relationship. If you do not have such a person or group, then either talk to someone this week or check in with your local youth worker and have him or her help you.

Further reading: Acts 2:42-47; Hebrews 10:24-25.

Endnotes

Day 5
1. Max Lucado, *When Christ Comes* (Nashville, TN: Work Publishing, 1999) pp. 21-22.

Day 14
1. Author unknown.

Day 16
1. William Barclay, *The Letter to the Romans* (Philadelphia: Westminster Press, 1975), p. 148.

Day 18
1. Albert Schweitzer, source unknown.

Day 19
1. William Barclay, *The Gospel of Matthew* (Philadelphia: Westminster Press, 1975), p. 326.

Day 21
1. Alexander Irvine, *My Lady of the Chimney Corner* (Belfast, Ireland: Apple Tree Press Ltd., 1981), n.p.

Day 27
1. Author Unknown, *The Spice of Life* (Norwalk, CT: C. R. Gibson, Co., 1971), p. 29.

Day 29
1. Anonymous.

Day 30
1. Orin D. Crain (publishing information unknown).

Day 33
1. F. B. Meyer (publishing information unknown).

Day 35
1. Tim Hansel, *You Gotta Keep Dancin'* (Elgin, IL: David C. Cook, 1985), p. 131.

Day 37
1. Billy Graham, source unknown.

Day 41
1. C. S. Lewis, *Mere Christianity* (New York: MacMillan, 1960), p. 56.

Day 42
1. Author unknown.

Day 43
1. Bill Bright, *Revolution Now* (San Bernardino, CA: Campus Crusade for Christ, 1969), pp. 186-187.

Day 44
1. Charles Swindoll, *Improving Your Serve* (Waco, TX: Word, 1981), p. 28.

Day 46
1. Tony Campolo, *You Can Make a Difference* (Waco, TX: Word, 1984), p. 14.

Day 47
1. Dwight Liles, "We Are an Offering" (Bug and Bear Music, Home Sweet Home Records Inc., 1984).

Day 48
1. Author unknown.

Day 49
1. Charles Colson, *Loving God* (Grand Rapids, MI: Zondervan, 1983), pp. 241-243. Used by permission.

JIM BURNS

is president of the YouthBuilders, a nonprofit organization that offers resources for youth workers, young people and parents, and provides training for youth ministries around the world. In addition to authoring many books, including the YouthBuilders curriculum series and *Addicted to God*, Jim also writes a column for *Campus Life* magazine and provides daily radio commentary with his YouthBuilders broadcasts, which are heard by over 2 million people.

For more information about YouthBuilders or for more information regarding videos, books, educational programs or other resources for parents, teens or youth workers, write or call:

YOUTHBUILDERS
32236 Paseo Adelante, Suite D
San Juan Capistrano, CA 92675
(800) 397-9725

More Resources to Help You Make a Difference

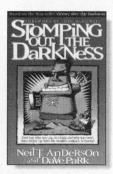

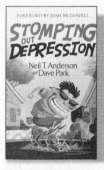

Wake 'Em Up!

This fresh-roasted blend of sizzling hot resources helps you turn youth meetings into dynamic events that kids look forward to. Successfully field-tested in youth groups and edited by youth expert **Jim Burns**, **Fresh Ideas** will wake 'em up and get your group talking.

Bible Study Outlines and Messages
ISBN 08307.18850

Case Studies, Talk Sheets and Starters
ISBN 08307.18842

Games, Crowdbreakers & Community Builders
ISBN 08307.18818

Illustrations, Stories and Quotes to Hang Your Message On
ISBN 08307.18834

Incredible Retreats
ISBN 08307.24036

Missions and Service Projects
ISBN 08307.18796

Skits and Dramas
ISBN 08307.18826

Worship Experiences
ISBN 08307.24044

Gospel Light